SHOW ME THE MONEY

EARNING MONEY

by J. P. Press

Consultant: Beth Gambro
Reading Specialist, Yorkville, Illinois

BEARPORT
PUBLISHING

Minneapolis, Minnesota

Teaching Tips

Before Reading

- Look at the cover of the book. Discuss the picture and the title.

- Ask readers to brainstorm a list of what they already know about earning money. What can they expect to see in the book?

- Go on a picture walk, looking through the pictures to discuss vocabulary and make predictions about the text.

During Reading

- Read for purpose. Encourage readers to think about earning money and the role money plays in their lives as they are reading.

- Ask readers to look for the details of the book. What are they learning about earning money?

- If readers encounter an unknown word, ask them to look at the sounds in the word. Then, ask them to look at the rest of the page. Are there any clues to help them understand?

After Reading

- Encourage readers to pick a buddy and reread the book together.

- Ask readers to name two things from the book they may be able to do to earn money. Go back and find the pages that tell about these things.

- Ask readers to write or draw something they learned about earning money.

Credits:

Cover and Title page, © SDI Productions/iStock; 3, © Tom Saga/Shutterstock; 5, © Summer Photographer/Shutterstock; 7, © iStock/SDI Productions; 8, © agrobacter/iStock; 9, © ravl/Shutterstock; 10–11, © Pixel-Shot/Shutterstock; 13, © SolStock/iStock; 14–15, © WiP-Studio/Shutterstock; 17, © New Africa/Shutterstock; 18, © Monkey Business Images/Shutterstock; 19, © Gilang Prihardono/Shutterstock; 21, © Koy_Hipster/Shutterstock; 22, © irin-k/Shutterstock, © Yobro10/iStock, © GlobalStock/iStock; 23, © kali9/iStock, © Alter-ego/Shutterstock, © Motortion Films/Shutterstock, © CoolimagesCo/Shutterstock, © SDI Productions/iStock

Library of Congress Cataloging-in-Publication Data

Names: Press, J. P., 1993- author.
Title: Earning money / J. P. Press, Consultant Beth Gambro, Reading
  Specialist, Yorkville, Illinois.
Description: Bearcub books. | Minneapolis : Bearport Publishing Company,
  2021. | Series: Show me the money | Includes bibliographical references
  and index.
Identifiers: LCCN 2020051878 (print) | LCCN 2020051879 (ebook) | ISBN
  9781647479008 (library binding) | ISBN 9781647479077 (paperback) | ISBN
  9781647479145 (ebook)
Subjects: LCSH: Money--Juvenile literature. | Work--Juvenile literature. |
  Finance, Personal--Juvenile literature.
Classification: LCC HG221.5 .P74 2021 (print) | LCC HG221.5 (ebook) | DDC
  332.024--dc23
LC record available at https://lccn.loc.gov/2020051878
LC ebook record available at https://lccn.loc.gov/2020051879

Copyright © 2022 Bearport Publishing Company. All rights reserved. No part of this publication may be reproduced in whole or in part, stored in any retrieval system, or transmitted in any form or by any means, electronic, mechanical, photocopying, recording, or otherwise, without written permission from the publisher.

For more information, write to Bearport Publishing, 5357 Penn Avenue South, Minneapolis, MN 55419. Printed in the United States of America.

Contents

A New Toy 4

Money Matters: Have a Yard Sale 22

Glossary 23

Index 24

Read More 24

Learn More Online........................ 24

About the Author 24

A New Toy

You want a new toy.

You find something fun at the store.

But wait!

Before you can get the toy, you need money.

Everything has a price.

You need to give money to get things.

One way to get money is to **earn** it.

Earning means doing a job to get something.

Doctors earn money when they make you better.

You can earn money, too!

There are many jobs you can do.

Start a **lemonade** stand!

Make lots of drinks.

Then, sell the lemonade to your friends and family.

What else can you do?

Have a **yard sale**!

First, ask a grown-up if it is okay.

Then, sell things you do not use.

People can buy your old toys and clothes.

14

Maybe you can earn money by doing extra jobs at home.

You can clean.

You can make food for your family.

There are lots of ways to earn money.

And there are lots of ways to **spend** money, too.

Think before you buy.

You may want a new bike.

But you need food and clothes.

Buy your needs before you buy your wants.

Be smart with the money you earn.

You worked hard and earned money.

Good job!

Now you can buy the new toy.

It can be fun to work for what you want.

Money Matters
Have a Yard Sale

1. Ask a grown-up if it is okay.

2. Plan a day for the sale. Tell your friends and family about it.

3. Find things to sell. Look for things you do not use. Make sure they are not dirty or **broken**.

4. Have your yard sale.

22

Glossary

broken in pieces or not working

earn to get something for work done

lemonade a drink made of lemons, sugar, and water

spend to use money to pay for something

yard sale a sale of used items held at the seller's home

Index

buy 12, 16, 19–20
lemonade stand 10
needs 19
price 6

sell 10, 12, 22
wants 19
yard sale 12, 22

Read More

Lindeen, Mary. *Earning Money (A Beginning-to-Read Book)*. Chicago: Norwood House Press, 2020.

Raij, Emily. *Earn Money (Earn It, Save It, Spend It!)*. North Mankato, MN: Pebble, 2020.

Learn More Online

1. Go to **www.factsurfer.com**
2. Enter "**Earning**" into the search box.
3. Click on the cover of this book to see a list of websites.

About the Author

J. P. Press likes to run and read. She earns money by working on books.